W9-BOL-221

REALLY ROTTEN TRUTH ABOUT
COMPOSTING

Jodie Mangor

Rourke
Educational Media

rourkeeducationalmedia.com

Scan for Related Titles and Teacher Resources

Before Reading:

Building Academic Vocabulary and Background Knowledge

Before reading a book, it is important to tap into what your child or students already know about the topic. This will help them develop their vocabulary, increase their reading comprehension, and make connections across the curriculum.

1. *Look at the cover of the book. What will this book be about?*
2. *What do you already know about the topic?*
3. *Let's study the Table of Contents. What will you learn about in the book's chapters?*
4. *What would you like to learn about this topic? Do you think you might learn about it from this book? Why or why not?*
5. *Use a reading journal to write about your knowledge of this topic. Record what you already know about the topic and what you hope to learn about the topic.*
6. *Read the book.*
7. *In your reading journal, record what you learned about the topic and your response to the book.*
8. *After reading the book complete the activities below.*

Content Area Vocabulary
Read the list. What do these words mean?

aerated
bacteria
castings
consumers
decomposers
ecosystem
energy
humus
ingest
landfills
microorganisms
nutrients
organic matter
recycling
static

After Reading:

Comprehension and Extension Activity

After reading the book, work on the following questions with your child or students in order to check their level of reading comprehension and content mastery.

1. *What happens in a compost pile?* (Summarize)
2. *How does chopping your compost material into smaller pieces affect the process?* (Infer)
3. *Why is compost described as black gold?* (Asking questions)
4. *What steps would you need to take to start composting at home or school?* (Text to self connection)
5. *Why would a government ban food waste from landfills?* (Asking questions)

Extension Activity

For one week, keep a list of the items you throw away that could be composted instead. Tally it up on the seventh day. How much waste went to a landfill that could have been turned into black gold instead? Now imagine that amount for every person on the planet. Ready to start composting yet?

Table of Contents

COMPOST: NATURE'S BLACK GOLD!

Instead of throwing food scraps away, you can turn them into a useful soil-like substance called compost.

The next time you finish a meal, take a look at your plate. Believe it or not, that crust of bread and pile of peas that didn't make it into your stomach have a lot of potential. They aren't just food scraps—they're ingredients for something precious. With just a little effort, scraps like these can be converted into a substance that people around the world value and depend on: black gold!

Black gold is another name for finished compost, a dark, crumbly mixture that is rich in minerals and other **nutrients**. It has the smell of fresh earth and holds onto moisture like a sponge. Compost can be mixed with soil to improve its quality and help plants to grow.

It's Alive! Or it Was ...

What is organic matter? It's anything that is—or ever was—alive. This includes plants and animals as well as their products (cotton and leather) and waste products (manure). All organic material can be composted, although some things take longer than others to decompose!

What is composting? It's nature's way of **recycling** organic matter and all the natural resources it contains.

Composting happens thanks to a diverse group of tiny organisms called **decomposers**. Decomposers range from single-celled **bacteria** to worms and other multi-celled organisms. These essential players in the web of life do the dirty work of cleaning up dead plants and animals and their wastes. They break down **organic matter** by eating and re-eating it (and each other!). This releases nutrients back into the environment and turns the matter into finished compost.

Food Chain Facts

Decomposers are an important part of every food chain. A food chain shows how energy and matter are transferred from one living creature to another. The first link in every chain is a producer, usually a plant, capable of making organic matter. Plants do this using the sun's energy, water, and carbon dioxide from the atmosphere in a process called photosynthesis. The next links are consumers, animals who get their food and energy by eating plants or other animals. When any of the links in the chain die, decomposers step in to break down their remains.

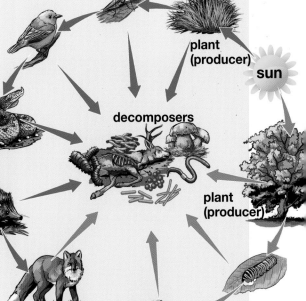

plant (producer)

sun

decomposers

plant (producer)

The world would be a different place without decomposers. Dead plants, trees and animals would just lie there. Manure piles would build up. More and more organic matter would clutter Earth's surface, and important resources wouldn't be recycled for future organisms to use.

Food chains combine and intertwine to create food webs like this one. As you can see, the web of life can be complicated, with different organisms often playing more than one role.

Decomposer vs. Scavenger

What's the difference between a decomposer and a scavenger? Scavengers eat dead things, breaking them into smaller pieces. Vultures, hyenas, and even raccoons are examples of scavengers. Decomposers such as bacteria and fungi take it one step further than scavengers: they convert organic matter into basic chemicals that can reenter the soil.

All organic matter is eventually turned into compost. When we humans get involved in composting, we can help speed up the process. By supplying decomposers with the right environment and balance of ingredients, what might take years in nature can happen in months or even weeks.

leaves,
woody materials

grass, food scraps,
manures

compost

water

air

compost happens

macro-organisms
(earthworms, insects, etc.)

micro-organisms
(bacteria, fungi, microbes)

Composting is amazingly good for the environment. When compost is mixed with soil, it adds nutrients vital for life. It also improves the soil's structure, making nutrients, water and oxygen more accessible. All of these things help plants grow. In turn, healthy, strong plants clean the air, help stabilize the soil and feed other creatures.

Sorting it Out

By sorting organic matter from other trash and composting them, we can reduce the amount of waste going into landfills—by 60 percent or more! When organic matter is dumped into a landfill, it produces methane, a powerful greenhouse gas. By keeping organic matter out of landfills, we can reduce the amount of methane. We can also save on the fuel and electricity used to transport and process wastes. All this, while creating a valuable resource!

PAPER   ORGANIC

Soil is teeming with life! The types and numbers of organisms found in soil are astounding, from **microorganisms** such as bacteria, actinomycetes, and fungi, to more complex creatures such as nematodes, earthworms, snails, and slugs! All of these soil-dwelling organisms can also be found in a compost pile. Whether in soil or compost, they are part of a system that cycles nutrients through the environment.

bacteria

fungal hyphae

protozoa

A Little Soil, A Lot of Life

What's in a teaspoon (about one gram) of soil? The answer depends on the type of soil. The more organic matter a soil has, the more life it can support.

Forest soils contain:
* up to one billion bacteria–about 40,000 different species!
* several hundred yards of fungal hyphae–fungi are measured in length
* several hundred thousand protozoa
* several hundred nematodes

Per square foot of soil, there are also
* 10–25,000 insects
* 10–50 earthworms

As organisms in the soil food web eat, grow, and move through the soil, they contribute to clean water, clean air, and healthy plants.

A compost pile is an **ecosystem** that includes all the living things in the pile, their environment and all the ways they interact. Within this ecosystem, there are many types of decomposers. They can be divided into three main groups, depending on what they eat:

- Primary **consumers** eat organic matter
- Secondary consumers eat primary consumers
- Tertiary consumers eat secondary consumers

This energy pyramid shows how energy is transferred through different types of decomposers in a compost pile:

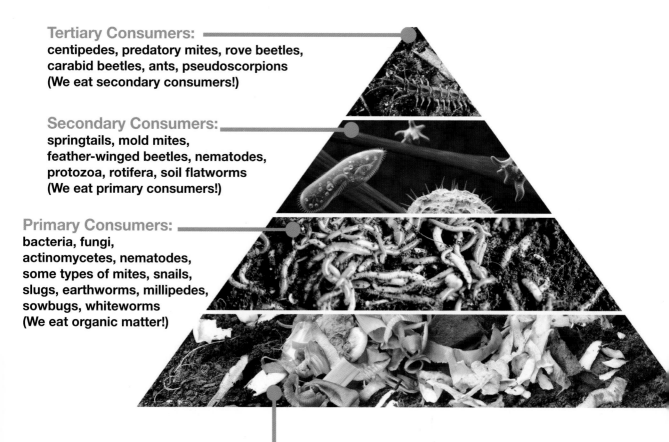

Tertiary Consumers:
centipedes, predatory mites, rove beetles, carabid beetles, ants, pseudoscorpions
(We eat secondary consumers!)

Secondary Consumers:
springtails, mold mites, feather-winged beetles, nematodes, protozoa, rotifera, soil flatworms
(We eat primary consumers!)

Primary Consumers:
bacteria, fungi, actinomycetes, nematodes, some types of mites, snails, slugs, earthworms, millipedes, sowbugs, whiteworms
(We eat organic matter!)

Organic Matter:
leaves, grass clippings, other plant debris, food scraps, dead animals, animal wastes.
(plant and animal residues)

It's mealtime! Compost starts with a pile of organic matter. Larger primary decomposers such as millipedes, sow bugs, worms, snails and slugs shred the matter as they eat. This creates more surface area for the real superstars of the compost pile: bacteria, actinomycetes and fungi. These tiny primary consumers do most of the decomposing.

MEET THE PLAYERS

Primary consumers (microbes)

Bacteria:
What we lack in size, we make up for in numbers! There are way more of us—a billion or so—in a compost pile than any other organisms, combined! You can find us at work throughout the composting process.

Actinomycetes:
We grow in long filaments just like fungi, but really we're a type of bacteria. Together with fungi, we tackle some of the toughest organic matter in the pile.

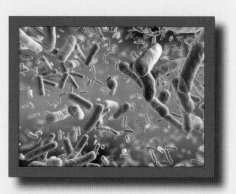

Fungi:
In compost, you'll find us mostly as long filaments called hyphae. We take acidic and dry organic matter such as lignins and cellulose and change it into something bacteria can eat.

Earthworms deserve a spot in the limelight. They eat organic matter and soil. Earthworm **castings** improve the structure of soil and are rich in nutrients such as nitrogen, calcium, magnesium, and phosphorus.

Earthworms are also secondary consumers, because they **ingest** microorganisms along with the organic matter.

MEET THE PLAYERS

More primary consumers:

Earthworm:
I am a star at turning organic matter into compost. I physically grind it into a fine paste in my gut and then chemically digest it. My castings–that's poop to you–are rich in nutrients.

Millipede:
My name means one thousand legs. I don't have quite that many, but I challenge you to count them all! Unlike my cousin the centipede, I'm a vegetarian and will roll up in a ball in the face of danger.

Sow Bug:
I'm a tiny relative of crayfish and lobsters. Because I have gills, I need to live in a moist environment. I'm on a vegetarian meal plan, all the way!

Slug:
I'll eat most types of organic matter, living or dead, and most types of vertebrates will eat me. There are also microorganisms that like to parasitize me. My slogan: eat or be eaten!

Before long, secondary consumers, including springtails, mold mites, nematodes, protozoa, and some types of beetles move into the pile to dine on primary consumers.

MEET THE PLAYERS

Secondary consumers:

Springtail:
I get my name from the spring-loaded structure tucked under my abdomen. I release it to project myself into the air. Molds and decaying matter are my eats of choice.

Mold mite:
Like the springtail, I'm common but often overlooked. You'll find me where it's moist and humid, eating my favorite food: mold!

Nematode:
Look for me in compost and in all types of soils. Under a magnifying glass, I look like a fine hair. We nematodes are amazingly diverse, with about 5,000 species living in soil and up to 500,000 species overall.

Protozoa:
I'm not a huge decomposer, but you can find me in the pile. I eat bacteria, fungi and some organic matter.

Feather-winged beetle:
I feed on fungal spores and am the smallest and one of the most common beetles in compost.

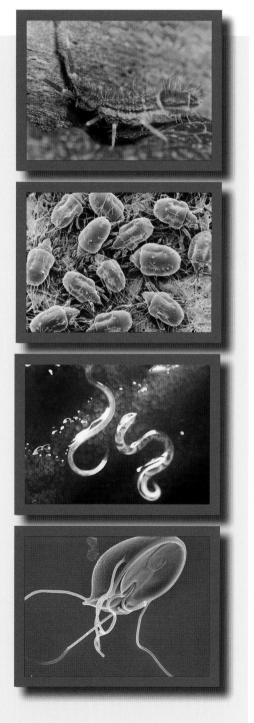

The compost pile is a prime hunting ground for tertiary consumers like centipedes, predatory mites, rove beetles, and pseudoscorpions. These predators like to feast on secondary consumers.

MEET THE PLAYERS

Tertiary consumers:

Centipede:
Look for me in the top few inches of the compost heap. I'm quick and deadly, with poison glands to paralyze my prey of small worms, larvae, insects and their larvae, and spiders.

Predatory mite:
I have eight legs like a spider and feed on nematodes, eggs, insect larvae, other mites and springtails.

Rove beetle:
I like nothing better than to eat springtails and nematodes in the dark, dank comfort of a compost pile.

Pseudoscorpion:
I look like a tiny scorpion with no tail. Nematodes, springtails, mites and worms— I'll eat 'em all! I have no eyes or ears, so I hunt by scent and sound, grabbing prey with my poisonous claws.

Who's Hiding in the Soil/Compost?
Hunting for Decomposers

What you'll need:

- several ½-cup (64 gram) samples of soil and/or compost taken from different depths
- light-colored trays or pans
- plastic spoons or wooden craft sticks

Optional:

- flashlight
- magnifying lens
- dissecting microscope
- paintbrush
- tweezers

What you'll do:

1. Place each sample on a separate tray.
2. Gently spread the sample over the surface of the tray, using the spoon or craft stick to move it around.
3. As you move the sample, look for organisms.
4. Experiment with shining the flashlight on the sample or looking through the magnifying lens to help you find organisms. The light color of the pan should make them easier to see. Keep in mind that many decomposers move away from bright light, not toward it.
5. To get a closer look, use the paintbrush or tweezers to gently transfer decomposers to a small, shallow container and observe them under a dissecting microscope if you have one.
6. Compare your samples. Which organisms did you find in your surface sample, and which did you find deeper inside the pile or the soil? What's different between the samples? What's the same?

Things to look for:

Worms, centipedes, millipedes, sowbugs, earwigs, spiders, beetles, snails, slugs, mites, insect larvae, springtails, and ants.

*Note: Bacteria and many other decomposers are too small to see with the naked eye, or even under a dissecting scope.

Food, air, water, and heat: Like all living things, decomposers have essential needs. Bacterial populations in particular will vary according to each of these factors.

Pile Population

There are many kinds of bacteria at work in the compost pile. Each type has preferences for certain foods and environmental conditions.

The pile is not uniform in temperature–the center is usually warmer than the outer layer–or in the amount of air, water, or food that's available (there may be apple peels over here, and yard waste over there). As conditions in the pile change, so do the populations of active bacteria.

FOOD: Eat it up. Yum!

As a group, decomposers are not picky eaters. Any organic matter will do, as long as it provides them with a source of **energy** and the basic building blocks they need to grow and reproduce. Still, it's best to provide decomposers with a balance of different types of materials. You can find a list of what to include—and what to leave out—on page 41.

Size Matters!

Whether you cut, chop, crunch or chip it up, smaller pieces of organic matter have more surface area than bigger ones. When there's more surface area, decomposers have more room to get to work. It's good to strive for some size variety, to help air flow through the pile!

This log and these wood chips are made of the same stuff—which do you think will turn to compost first?

Air: To Air, or Not to Air?

When it comes to compost, there's a clear answer to this question! The amount of air, or more specifically, oxygen (O) circulating through a compost pile has a direct effect on how the pile functions.

Aerobes, microorganisms that grow in the presence of oxygen, make compost quickly and efficiently in a well-**aerated** pile. Anaerobes, microorganisms that live in the absence of oxygen, do the decomposing when there's no or low oxygen. Anaerobic composting is usually a slow and smelly process!

Homemade compost bins often have the best air circulation, while store-bought bins have locking lids to keep out unwanted wildlife.

There's Air in There

Although soil appears solid, air moves freely in and out of its surface. Large invertebrates, such as earthworms, ants, termites, and beetles, burrow through soil. This creates spaces that air and water can move into and through.

Water: Keeping It Moist

To stay alive and thrive, bacteria, fungi, and invertebrates need a certain amount of moisture. They're happiest in compost that has a moisture level of 40 to 60 percent, so that it feels damp to the touch. At moisture levels below 35 percent, decomposers can't work as fast, and below 30 percent they stop decomposing altogether. On the other hand, if the compost pile becomes too wet, above 60 percent or so, it can lead to stinky, anaerobic conditions.

Heat: The Fast Track to Compost

One of the ways we can make compost happen faster is by helping it reach ideal temperatures for maximum decomposition. As decomposers—especially bacteria—break organic matter down into less complex molecules, energy is released. The faster the decomposers work, the hotter it gets, and the hotter it gets, the faster they work!

To get a pile to heat up and stay warm, you have to have the right mix of organic matter, air, and water. But watch out! If the pile gets too hot (above 65°C or 149°F) it will kill many decomposers. To cool down an overheating pile, turn it with a pitchfork.

Even without heat, organic matter will eventually break down, but it can take a long, long time—as it sometimes does on the forest floor.

Composting has three temperature phases:

Phase 1: Moderate temperatures of 77–104°F (25–40°C). Microorganisms that thrive at these temperatures break down readily available sugars and starches. This activity causes the temperature of the pile to rise.

Phase 2: High temperatures of 104–158°F (40–70°C). Heat-loving bacteria take over, decomposing proteins, fats, and complex carbohydrates like cellulose.

Phase 3: The pile cools back to 77–104°F (25–40°C). The last of the high-energy compounds are used up. As the temperature starts to fall, bacteria that thrive at moderate temperatures become active again. They decompose any remaining materials.

Composting is a process of chemical changes. As decomposers eat organic matter, they break it into smaller, more basic units. Organic matter is made up of many types of organic compounds. Organic compounds are substances that are made from carbon atoms and other chemical elements, joined by chemical bonds. Proteins, fats, and

The complex organic matter in this bin is being converted into simple molecules.

carbohydrates are all types of organic compounds.

Decomposers break proteins into amino acids, fats into fatty acids, and carbohydrates into sugar molecules. These and other chemical changes free up elements like carbon and nitrogen so that they can continue cycling through the food web and the environment.

Chemical or Physical?

Organic matter goes through physical and chemical changes in a compost pile.

A physical change is a change that doesn't affect internal structures, such as when a stick is broken into smaller pieces.

A chemical change is change in which chemical bonds are created or destroyed, such as a carbohydrate being broken down into simple sugars with different characteristics.

21

Carbon and nitrogen are two of the most important chemical players in the compost pile. Decomposers need plenty of carbon and nitrogen to work and grow. Because only a certain amount of these resources exist on Earth, we depend on cycles to keep them available to us and all other living creatures.

In a compost pile, decomposers use carbon-containing compounds as an energy source. Some good sources of carbon are leaves, brush, sawdust and wood chips. You can tell that organic matter is high in carbon if it is brown, dry, and brittle.

6	12.0107
C	
Carbon	

Carbon (C):

Carbon is the fourth most common chemical element in the universe. All living things are made from carbon. It can also be found in the ocean, the atmosphere, and soil. Like other elements, it cycles from place to place, being used and reused in different forms.

This combination of fruit and carbon-rich leaves will compost naturally on the soil surface, returning nutrients to the soil from which they grew.

The Carbon Cycle

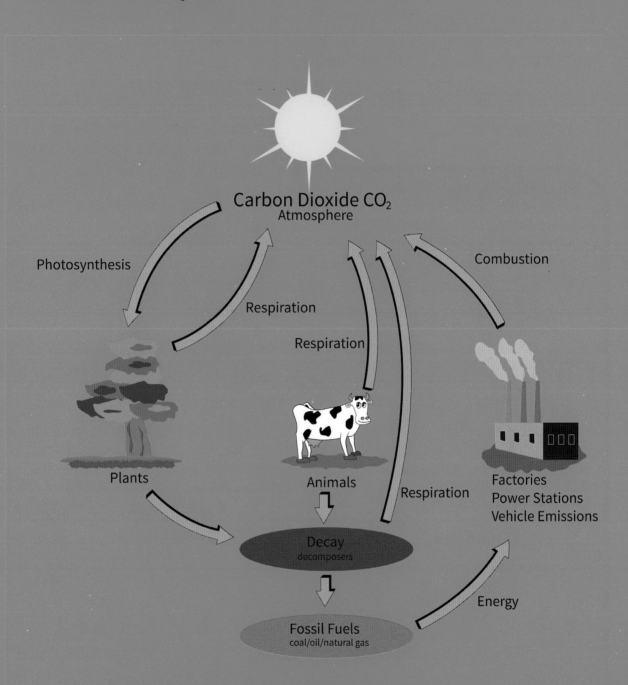

Plants use carbon from carbon dioxide (CO2) in the atmosphere to make sugars. These sugars move through the web of life until they are turned back into CO2 and are released into the atmosphere.

High levels of nitrogen can be found in food wastes, grass clippings, and manure. You can tell that organic matter is high in nitrogen if it is green and moist.

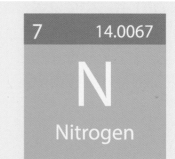

Nitrogen (N):
All living things need this chemical element to grow and reproduce. It is an essential part of proteins, DNA and RNA.

The Nitrogen Cycle

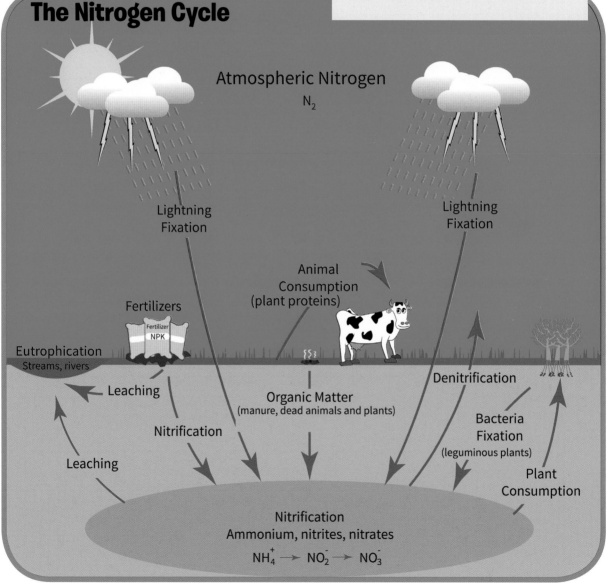

Like carbon, nitrogen is constantly being cycled through the air and Earth.

The Right Balance

Just like people, bacteria need a balanced diet. To keep these little decomposers happy, and make fast, hot compost, the levels of carbon and nitrogen in the compost pile should be at a ratio of about 30 parts carbon to one part nitrogen. This can be achieved by mixing about three parts green stuff like grass or plants with one part woody brown stuff like leaves, straw, or woodchips.

The right mix leads to a healthy compost pile.

Material	Carbon/Nitrogen Ratio
Food scraps	15:1
Grass clippings	19:1
Coffee grounds	20:1
Straw	80:1
Newspaper	170:1
Sawdust	500:1

A Perfect Meal

Maple leaves have a 30:1 ratio of carbon to nitrogen. This makes them a perfect meal for many decomposers. With the right amount of water and air, decomposers can turn them into compost in just a few short weeks.

25

Good Rot or Not? How Fast Do Different Combinations of Materials Decompose?

What you'll need:

* several quart-size containers (empty yogurt containers work well)
* greens: kitchen scraps, grass clippings
* browns: leaves, straw, wood chips or shavings
* some water
* a trowel
* a marker and/or tape to label the containers

What you'll do:

1. With the trowel or spade, chop the food and other organic material into small pieces. Leave some large pieces in for comparison.
2. Fill one container ¾ full with browns only.
3. Fill a second container ¾ full with greens only.
4. Fill the third container ¾ full with a mix of half greens and half browns.
5. Add just enough water to each container so that the contents are moist but not wet.
6. Keep the containers outside, loosely covered with plastic lids or pieces of cardboard; this experiment works best in warm weather.
7. Every few days, open up the containers, mix the contents with a trowel, and if needed, add just enough water to keep the contents moist.
8. After two to four weeks, evaluate what's happened.
9. Study the contents of each container. Take note of temperature, odor, texture, and weight. Do they smell? Are they decomposing? Which container's contents appeared to compost the most?

Here's a guide you can compare your results to:

* too little carbon = wet, dense, smelly pile
* too much carbon = dry pile, slow decomposition
* too little nitrogen = microbes won't grow, slow decomposition
* too much nitrogen = microbes make smelly ammonia gas
* a good balance of carbon and nitrogen = organic matter decomposes nicely, no awful odors

Smells: The Good, the Bad, and the Ugly

Compost gets a bad rap for being smelly. It's true, it can smell bad, but only if the pile is off balance. Having too much nitrogen or not enough oxygen are two conditions that cause bad smells.

The smells come from chemical compounds produced by decomposers. A healthy, well-balanced compost pile will have a pleasant, earthy smell.

What's that Smell?

As they break down organic matter, anaerobic bacteria excrete smelly compounds, including:

- hydrogen sulfide gas (H_2S) which smells like rotten eggs
- ammonia (NH_3)
- amines like cadaverine, and putrescine (putrid, fishy offensive odors)

So where does the good smell of aerobic compost come from? Credit has been given to a chemical called geosmin, which is produced by actinomycetes.

Actinomycetes are a type of bacteria

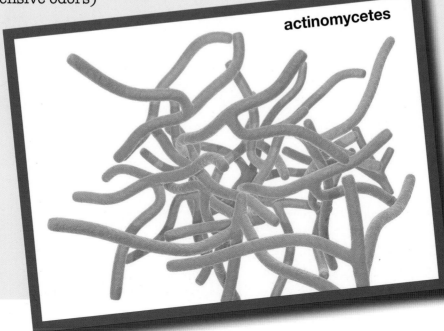

actinomycetes

What the Heck is Humus?

It takes time, but eventually decomposers will reach a point where they've used up pretty much all the organic compounds they can in a compost pile. If you wait long enough, you'll end up with a material called **humus**. This brown/black, crumbly, sponge-like material is a type of finished compost.

If humus were to be decomposed further, which can happen, but v-e-r-y slowly, it would be turned into very simple inorganic substances.

Nutrient-rich humus, or black gold, can hold several times its weight in water.

COMPOST, COMPOST ONE AND ALL!

Composting can happen at different levels, from a backyard compost pile to giant facilities that compost an entire city's organic wastes, to international efforts!

International Compost Awareness Week
International Compost Awareness Week (ICAW) is celebrated every year during the first full week of May.

By sorting out materials that can be recycled or composted, we can reduce the amount of matter we put into landfills.

Small But Significant

With just a little know-how, small scale home composting can be easy and a great way to get rid of yard waste and kitchen scraps.

If you have room, you can set up a bin in your backyard. If you live in a place without enough outdoor space, don't despair! There are ways to compost indoors, including digester composting (see page 37) and vermicomposting (see page 38).

Small is good, but too small won't get the job done. To be able to reach the desired temperature levels, a compost pile should be at least 1 cubic yard (or meter) in size.

When composting at home, collect kitchen scraps in a container that can easily be carried out and emptied into the compost bin.

What a Waste!

American families throw out about 25 percent of all the food they buy, and overall, 40 percent of food in the United States never gets eaten. This is equivalent to more than 20 pounds of food per person every month. Almost all of this organic waste ends up in a landfill.

When we throw organic waste into landfills, we break natural resource cycles and keep limited natural resources out of the environment. We also increase the amount of methane, a greenhouse gas that contributes to global warming, that is being released into the environment.

What can we do to keep organic matter out of landfills?

- Pay more attention to what we do with the food we buy.
- Change wasteful habits.
- Keep food from becoming waste in the first place.
- Compost at home!

Community Compost

People can also set up compost operations on a medium scale. Across the nation, communities are finding ways to compost more of their organic wastes. Many schools now have compost programs.

Community Composting

The Finger Lakes Grassroots Festival of Music and Dance is a great example of community composting. Volunteers from Cornell Cooperative Extension collect food waste and compostable plates, cups and utensils from food vendors and festival goers, and compost it. The project has grown over the years, and so have the compost piles!

From 1995 to 2009, the program kept over 55 tons of food waste from the landfill, tripling the amount it collected each year.

Who Has the Biggest Pile of Them All?

Large municipal and commercial composting operations are run by operators who understand the biology and chemistry of composting. It is important to keep these composting systems in balance so that the composting happens quickly and at temperatures high enough to kill disease-causing organisms and weed seeds.

Municipalities and communities benefit from organized large scale and city composting programs.

Mandatory Composting

What happens when an entire city composts? San Francisco, California, has the United States' first mandatory composting law. Together with its recycling efforts, the city keeps 80 percent of what it throws away out of the landfill. Other cities are following San Francisco's lead in reducing organic waste. Currently, more than 150 American cities offer curbside municipal compost pickup.

International Composting

We have a problem with waste. According to the Environmental Protection Agency, there's more food going into U.S. **landfills** than any other material, including paper or plastic. Other nations face similar situations. Fortunately, people around the world are stepping up their composting efforts to help the environment.

Composting Around the World

- In South Korea, food waste has been banned from landfills since 2005.
- Many European countries compost on the municipal level. Some top composting countries in the European Union are Austria, the Netherlands, France, Spain, and Germany.
- India has 70 cities with composting facilities, and that number is growing.
- Canada has the largest compost system for handling both residential solid waste and sewage biosolids in North America. It's big enough to cover about eight football fields.
- Large-scale composting facilities can now be found around the world, including in Pakistan, Qatar, Egypt, Mexico, South Africa, China, Indonesia and Brazil.

THE ART OF COMPOSTING

There's more than one way to make compost. The four main types of home compost systems are static systems, dynamic systems, digesters, and vermiculture (also known as worm ranching).

Static composting takes the least amount of effort. After building a pile of balanced ingredients, you just leave it there to do its thing. Green and brown (carbon and nitrogen) materials can be layered onto the pile at different times, with oldest materials at the bottom and newest on top.

It's Easy!

A compost bin can be made of many things—wood, wire, or even plastic! Remember: airflow within and around the pile is important.

You never need to add decomposers to a compost system. They're already everywhere; in the air, the soil and on the organic matter to be composted. Give them food, and they will come!

Dynamic composting is a lot like the static system, but involves a little more effort. By keeping track of the pile's temperature and occasionally adding water and turning it with a pitchfork, this method is hotter and faster than static composting.

In dynamic composting, mixing or turning a compost pile introduces more air and blends the browns and greens together. This speeds up the composting process.

Digesters are enclosed compost systems. They stand apart from other compost systems because they are designed to use anaerobic bacteria to decompose food scraps. Digesters are the only small-scale system that can handle meat, bones, and some dairy products.

Automated Digesters

There are now automated food digesters on the market that claim to decompose most waste food into high quality compost in just 24 to 48 hours! You need to buy and add microorganisms to these machines. Then they cycle through different temperature ranges to speed up the composting process. Some digesters are small and portable, making them an option if you don't have a backyard.

Anaerobic bacteria are responsible for eating the organic matter in a digester.

Vermicomposting is a worm-powered compost method that can be done indoors. Vermicomposting is simple: Worms eat food scraps and poop out the remains in the form of nutrient-rich castings. But be careful—you'll need worms that can handle warmer, crowded conditions and the constant addition of organic matter. Red Wiggler worms (scientific name: *Eisenia fetida*) are often used for vermicomposting.

Make Your Own Vermicompost System

To set up a vermicompost system, you'll need four things:

- a container at least 1½ square feet and about 16 inches deep
- some sort of 'bedding' for the worms – damp shredded newspaper works great!
- worm food: kitchen scraps
- 500 to 1,000 composting worms– they'll need to be fed every three to seven days (always bury the food under paper!)

You'll be able to harvest worm castings after three to six months.

Setting up a compost pile of your own is easy. The first step is finding a spot to put it. An ideal location is:

- Shady
- Within reach of a water hose
- Out of the way, yet convenient
- Spacious
- Well drained

Many people use the back corner of their yard.

If you don't have an outdoor spot for a compost pile, you may want to consider setting up a worm bin inside.

Compost piles don't require a lot of space.

Setting Up Your Own Compost Pile

What you'll need:

- 4 x 12-foot (1.22 x 3.65-meter) of 1.5 inch (3.81-centimeter) mesh wire fencing
- pieces of bendable wire (you can use paper clips)
- sticks up to three feet (about one meter), in length
- greens: kitchen scraps, grass clippings
- browns: leaves, straw, wood chips or shavings
- pitchfork
- water
- patience and time!

What you'll do:

1. Form the wire into a cylinder that's three to four feet (.92 to 1.22 meters) in diameter and four feet (1.22 meters) high. Overlap the edges by an an inch or two (a few centimeters) and secure them with pieces of wire at the top, middle and bottom so that the cylinder is held together.
2. Place broken sticks at the bottom of your bin to create some pockets for air.
3. Place a three to four-inch (7 to 10-centimeter) layer of carbon-rich brown materials like hay, straw, or old leaves over the sticks.
4. Add nitrogen-rich green materials like grass clippings, manure, table scraps. Spread them in a thin layer on top of the browns, leaving an outer border of browns.
5. Completely cover the greens with another layer of browns.
6. No need to add microbes—they are already in the air, on the organic matter, or waiting nearby!
7. Every time you add a layer of greens, cover them with browns. Don't let any greens show through, as they can attract pests to the pile.
8. Add enough water to the pile to keep it moist, but don't overwater—more water means less space for air.
9. Continue adding layers of greens and browns until your bin is full.
10. Between adding layers, cover the pile with a tarp. This will keep rain out and moisture in.
11. When the pile reaches a height of three feet (about one meter), turn with a pitchfork to mix and add air to the pile. If you turn your pile regularly, every week or two, it will compost faster.

Here are some pointers on what can go into a compost pile—and what shouldn't.

YES!
- hay or straw
- leaves and pine needles
- kitchen scraps (egg shells, bread, vegetable and fruit scraps, coffee grounds)
- animal manure from your vegetarian pet (no dog, cat, pig, or human poop!)
- yard waste
- sawdust
- wood chips
- shredded black and white newspaper

NO!
(These things can attract animal pests or spread disease.)
- animal-based products such as meats, oils, fish, dairy products, and bones. Rats and raccoons like these!
- weed seeds
- diseased or insect-infested plants
- plants treated with herbicide
- dog, cat, pig or human poop. Poop from meat eaters can contain disease-causing organisms, or pathogens, so it's best to compost it in a large compost system that heats up higher and longer than a small-scale compost pile.

Can Carcasses be Composted?

Even though they are made of organic matter, dead animals should be kept out of a home compost pile.

However, it's perfectly fine to put them into a larger compost system capable of killing disease-causing organisms. In fact, composting carcasses can be a practical and inexpensive way to get rid of dead farm animals and road kill while recycling nutrients.

Is It Done Yet?

Finished compost or humus is like super food for plants. But using compost before it is ready can actually be harmful to plants. Materials that have not been decomposed enough can make nutrients even less available, and can also contain plant pests, weed seed, and diseases.

Finished compost should look and smell like rich, dark earth. There should be no visible bits of food in it.

Activity

The Jar Test

The Jar test is an easy way to test if compost is ready to use.

What you'll need:
- A small glass jar with a lid (like an old, washed out jam jar)
- 1 spoonful (14.79 milliliters) of the compost you want to test
- 1-2 spoonfuls (14.79- 29.58 milliliters) of water

What you'll do:
1. Spoon the compost into the jar.
2. Add enough water to make it soggy. Screw the lid onto the jar.
3. After a week, open the jar (carefully!) and take a whiff. If it smells nice, like wet earth, then the compost is done. If it smells bad, then there is still some organic matter than needs to finish decomposing. The smell is made by anaerobic bacteria as they try to finish the job.

What Compost Can Do for You and Your Plants

When you add compost to a garden, you are helping to complete a food web. When plants have access to nitrogen, phosphorous, potassium, and other nutrients in compost, they will grow faster and be healthier.

When you eat plants and vegetables grown in compost, you too reap the benefits of all these nutrients!

There are many things you can do with compost. Mix it with the soil in your garden. Sprinkle it on lawns, use it as mulch around trees and bushes, or add it to your potted plants.

Compost versus chemical fertilizers you can buy in the store

Outcome	Compost	Chemical fertilizer
Causes plants to grow more and faster	Yes	Yes
Improves organic matter content	Yes	
Encourages healthy root growth	Yes	
Can contaminate groundwater with excess nitrates		Yes
Made from non renewable resources		Yes
Harmful to environment		Yes
Harmful to human health		Yes

When it comes to the health of our environment, making compost is like hitting pay dirt! Composting reduces waste, reuses organic materials, and promotes healthy farming practices. It's a clean, safe, sustainable way to take care of organic waste.

Advantages of Composting

- It increases organic matter in soils
- It adds airspace to the soil
- It increases the soil's ability to hold onto moisture
- It promotes healthy root systems in plants
- It improves vitamin and mineral content in plants that grow in it
- It helps control soil erosion
- It helps balance the pH of soil
- It helps reduce greenhouse gases
- It reduces the amount of waste we funnel into landfills
- It keeps important nutrients cycling in the environment

And the list goes on!

DIG IN TO MAKE A DIFFERENCE

Composting is a great way to make a difference and have a positive effect on the environment. If your family already composts, offer to help. Add your food scraps to the compost pile at least once every few days. If your family doesn't compost, share what you've learned in this book. Enlist their help to start a compost pile, or depending on where you live, a worm bin for vermicomposting. Then get busy, collecting those greens and browns.

You also might want to look into what's happening in your school cafeteria. If your school doesn't already have a composting program, talk to your teacher about starting one.

TIMELINE

2320–2120 BCE: Someone from the Akkadian Empire scratched the first written account of composting into clay tablets.

234–149 BCE: A Roman named Marcus Porcius Cato wrote about composting animal manure and plant matter, and even mentioned vermicomposting!

50 BCE: Cleopatra of Ancient Egypt made worms sacred because of their composting abilities.

100 to 0 BCE: In Ancient China, Fan Sheng-Chih Shu wrote about adding cooked bones, manure and silkworm debris to soil.

900–1100 CE: The Arab Ibn al Awam described ingredients for making compost.

1621: Native Americans taught pilgrims how to add fish remains to soil to help crops grow.

1760: George Washington wrote in his diary about experimenting with composting systems.

Early 1900s: Many farmers switched to using chemical fertilizers instead of compost.

Late 1900s to present: Interest in composting has been renewed! People around the world are composting at all different scales.

GLOSSARY

aerated (air-ATE-ed): supplied with air

bacteria (bak-TEER-ee-uh): very small, single-celled living things that can be found almost everywhere

castings (KAST-ings): materials that have passed through a worm's digestive tract

consumers (kuhn-SOO-mers): organisms that feed on other organisms

decomposers (dee-kuhm-POZE-uhrs): organisms that feed on dead plant or animal matter

ecosystem (EE-koh-sis-tuhm): a community of living things interacting with their environment

energy (EN-ur-jee): usable power

humus (HYOO-muhs): a brown or black material found in soil that comes from decaying plants and animals

ingest (in-JEST): to take something into the body

landfills (LAND-fils): large areas where wastes are buried

microorganisms (mye-kroh-OR-guh-niz-uhms): extremely small living things that can only be seen with a microscope

nutrients (NOO-tree-uhnts): substances that living things need to live, grow, and be healthy

organic matter (or-GAN-ik MAT-uhr): material from or produced by living things

recycling (re-SYE-kling): processing something so it can be used again

static (STAT-ik): showing little change

INDEX

SHOW WHAT YOU KNOW

1) Name at least five organisms that live in a typical outdoor compost bin.
2) How do decomposers help to recycle organic matter?
3) Why is it important that more than one kind of decomposer be in the pile?
4) What four ingredients do decomposers need to be fast and efficient in making compost?
5) What are some ways that composting improves the environment?

WEBSITES TO VISIT

http://hdl.handle.net/1813/11656

www.pbslearningmedia.org/resource/tdc02.sci.life.oate.decompose/
  decomposers

http://pbskids.org/dragonflytv/show/wormfarm.html

ABOUT THE AUTHOR

Jodie Mangor is a trained Master Composter with a passion for microbes and a compost pile of her own. She puts her degrees in microbiology, environmental science, and molecular biology to work by editing papers for publication in scientific journals. Her stories, poems, and articles have appeared in a variety of children's magazines, and she has authored audio tour scripts for high-profile museums and tourist destinations around the world. Many of these tours are for kids. She lives in Ithaca, New York, with her family.

Meet The Author!
www.meetREMauthors.com

www.rourkeeducationalmedia.com

PHOTO CREDITS: Cover and title page © background © maodoltee, dirt pile © Imageman, food scraps 2 © into, worm © Kuttelvaserova Stuchelova, stamp graphic on cover and as chapter heads © TanjaJovicic.; page 4 top © Peter Burnett, bottom © sarasang, page 5 © LSkywalker; page 6 food web © Jakub Pavlinec, Paul Aniszewski, imagestalk, rck_953, Steve Byland, Volha Ahranovich, Titanchik, Jakub Pavlinec, yuris, GRASS, chantal de bruijne, Kokhanchikov, Fedorov Oleksiy; page 6 vulture © MattiaATH, page 7 leaves © Alexander Kazantsev, food scraps © Mona Makela, compost bucket © Sarah Marchant, earthworm © Maryna Pleshkun, fungi © Kichigin, water and air icons © Vectomart;; page 8 © LiudmylaSupynska, page 9 top © AlexRaths, middle © Kichigin, bottom and page 10 © Wire_man; page 10 pyramid bottom © sanddebeautheil, earthworm layer © Bernhard Richter, top © Imfoto, page 11 top © spanteldotru, middle © sciencepics, bottom © Derris Lund; page 12 earthworm © Maryna Pleshkun, millipede © Ryan M. Bolton, Sow Bug © PHOTO FUN, slug © Szasz-Fabian Jozsef, page 13 Springtail © Henrik Larsson, mold mite courteous of Agricultural Research Service, USDA, Nematode and Protozoa courtesy Source:CDC's Public Health Image Library, Feather-winged beetle source Ptenidium pusillum (Gyllenhal, 1808); page 14 centipede © TairA, predatory mite © Mick Talbot, Rove beetle © Katarina Christenson, Pseudoscorpion © Henrik Larsson; page 16 and 17 full page © Joan Ramon Mendo Escoda, page 16 inset © addax, page 17 inset left © somsak suwanput, inset right © sherwood, page 18 left © Evan Lorne, right © Alison Hancock, page 19 © Krit Leoniz; page 20 © Sustainable Sanitation Alliance, page 21 © BMJ; page 22 © Alexandra Giese, diagrams page 23 and 24 © photoiconix, page 25 grass © Luisa Leal Photography, leaves © Luisa Leal Photography and Linda Vostrovska, maple leaf © Planner; page 28 © 13Imagery, page 29 © Michael Warwick, page 30 © Patty Orly, page 31 © De Visu; page 32-33 © Gary Whitton, page 32 bottom © aspen rock; page 34-35 © JurateBuiviene; page 36 © Elena Elisseeva, page 37 © kallerna, wikimedia; page 38 © BERNATSKAYA OXANA, p39 © Chrislofotos; page 41 photo © sanpom, x-mark © samiph222; page 42 © Madlen, page 43 © Gayvoronskaya_Yana; page 44 © Jamie Hooper

Edited by: Keli Sipperley

Cover and Interior design by: Nicola Stratford   www.nicolastratford.com

Library of Congress PCN Data

Really Rotten Truth About Composting / Jodie Mangor
(Let's Explore Science)
  ISBN 978-1-68191-392-6 (hard cover)
  ISBN 978-1-68191-434-3 (soft cover)
  ISBN 978-1-68191-473-2 (e-Book)
Library of Congress Control Number: 2015951559

Printed in the United States of America, North Mankato, Minnesota

Also Available as:

ROURKE'S e-Books